W9-BSY-625

WACKY WORD GAMES

TO PLAY WITH YOUR FRIENDS

BY ALESHA SULLIVAN

CAPSTONE PRESS
a capstone imprint

Blazers Books are published by Capstone Press,
1710 Roe Crest Drive, North Mankato, Minnesota 56003
www.mycapstone.com

Library of Congress Cataloging-in-Publication Data
Library of Congress Cataloging-in-Publication data is available on the Library of Congress
website.
ISBN 978-1-5435-0338-8 (library binding)
ISBN 978-1-5435-0347-0 (eBook PDF)

Editorial Credits:
Mandy Robbins, editor; Eric Gohl, media researcher;
Tori Abraham, production specialist

Photo Credits:
Shutterstock: Aaron Amat, 19 (basketball), Askolds Berovskis, 11 (background), Bilda-
gentur Zoonar GmbH, 25, EtiAmmos, 13 (icicles), Gyorgy Barna, 20, H.Tanaka, 30, irin-k,
10, Janis Blums, 23, kazoka, 13 (pot), M. Unal Ozmen, 19 (ice cream), Mega Pixel, 26–27,
Mendenhall Olga, 11 (woodchuck), mikeledray, 16 (hat), Ollyy, 8–9, pathdoc, 15, pkproject,
7, saiko3p, 19 (banana peel), SLP_London, 21, Tara Swan, 16 (lamb), TFoxFoto, 29 (cow),
zcw, 4, Zhou Eka, 29 (tire)

Printed and bound in the United States of America.
010877S18

TABLE OF CONTENTS

WORD PLAY

Say this as fast as you can:

clean clams crammed
in clean cans

Tricky, right? Word games involve making up or guessing words based on a set of rules. Wind your way through word scrambles, tongue twisters, and spoonerisms. These brainy, zany word games are perfect to play with friends!

To find answers to the wacky word games in this book, turn to page 31!

CHAPTER 1

TONGUE TWISTERS

Suzie sells seashells on the seashore.

Say that three times fast! A tongue twister is a string of words that is difficult to say quickly. See if you can master these silly sentences.

TRICKY TWISTERS

1. A proper copper coffee pot

2. Flies fly but a fly flies.

1. Noisy **boys** enjoy noisy toys. But noisy boys enjoying noisy toys are annoying.

2. I can think of six **thin** things and six **thick** things too.

3. Gleeful **gray geese** are in the **green grass grazing.**

TROUBLING TWISTERS

1. A big black **bug** bit a big black **bear.** But where is the **big black bear** that the big black bug **bit?**

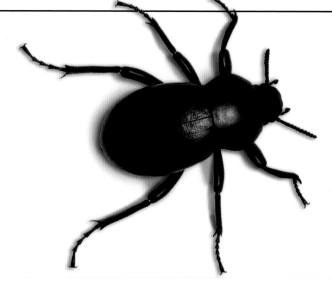

2. Peter Piper picked a peck of **pickled peppers.** If Peter Piper picked a peck of pickled peppers, how many pickled peppers did **Peter Piper** pick?

3. How much **wood** would a woodchuck **chuck** if a woodchuck could **chuck wood**? He would chuck, he would, as much as he could, and chuck as much wood, as a **woodchuck** would if a woodchuck could chuck wood.

CHAPTER 2

SPOONERISMS

Do you sometimes flip the beginning parts of a couple of words by accident? There's a name for that — a spoonerism. Time to have spun with foonerisms!

See if you can solve these spoonerisms with your friends!

LEVEL: EASY

1. It's roaring pain.

2. A well-boiled icicle

LEVEL: SEMI-EXPERT

1. I'm shout of the hour.

2. I bit my hunny phone.

3. This is the pun fart.

FUN FACT

The word "spoonerism" came from a reverend named William Spooner. One day in chapel, Spooner meant to announce the name of a hymn called "Conquering Kings Their Titles Take." But what came out was, "Kinquering Kongs Their Titles Take."

LEVEL: INSANE IN THE BRAIN!

1. Marry **hatter** ladle limb.

Itch fleas worse widest snore.

An **ever** war debt Marry win,

door limb worse shorter **gore**.

2. Oiled Mortar Harbored

win tooter **cardboard**

tow gutter pair darker boon.

Wind sheet gut **dare**,

duck cardboard worse blare,

end **soda** pair dark hat noon.

CHAPTER 3

WHATCHA' SAYIN'?

"Whole league how!" If you said that out loud, you probably heard, "Holy cow!" This game groups words together that don't make sense at first. But say them slowly, and listen carefully to figure out the phrase.

LEVEL: BEGINNER

1. Abe **An An** Appeal

2. Zola Reek **Lips**

3. **My** Cull Chore Den

4. Jog Clay Die **Scream**

LEVEL: INTERMEDIATE

1. Aid Us Sinner Owe **Hoses**

2. Thick Hull **Foam** Heck Sicko

3. Dune Hot **Feed** Than Hymn Hulls.

4. Creased My **Sieve**

5. Dawn Tall Quit Chore **Mile** Full!

LEVEL: GET A CROWN, BECAUSE YOU'RE THE KING!

1. Freeze Age Ha Leak Good Fell Owe.

2. Dawned Hay Guinea Chants His.

3. Ash Hold Hurt Hook Rye Yawn

4. Check Can Tub Ends Talk

5. Around Dove Apple Laws

CHAPTER 4

WILD WORD CHALLENGES

Homophones are tricky words. They sound the same. But they are spelled differently and have different meanings. Can you pick out the misused homophones in these sentences?

HOLY HOMOPHONES

1. Did **ewe** by a **serf** bored?

2. Eye **guest** ewe wood **bee** they're.

3. The **tied** rows for **feat**.

FUN FACT

The word "homophone" comes from the Greek language. In Greek *homo* means "same," and *phone* means "sound."

SCRAMBLED UP

What if you threw a word up in the air and let the letters fall where they may? You would have a word scramble! See if you can untangle these letters to make real word.

1. R O F E E B

2. P R E P Z I

3.

G E L A
T H U R

4.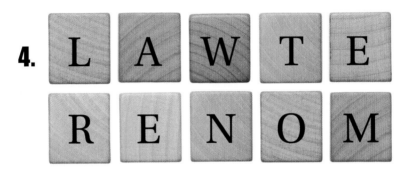

L A W T E
R E N O M

5.

T A F E T
R I C C E I

MAGICALLY MULTIPLYING WORDS

How many more words can you squeeze out of just one? Grab your friends, set a time limit, and see who can come up with the most words. Take the following word, for example:

irresistible

Can you think of any more words other than what's listed here?

1. IT

2. REST

3. BEST

4. LEST

5. BIT

6. SISTER

7. BITE

8. SIT

9. BLISS

10. STEER

11. STEEL

Now it's your turn! Get your friends together. See who can make the most words out of jellyfish, scatterbrained, or dictionary. Or get out your own dictionary, and come up with even more wild, wacky words!